Going Home

Going Home

Margaret Mayer Simon

Kravitz & Sons
INNOVATORS IN PUBLISHING, MARKETING AND ADVERTISING

Kravitz and Sons LLC
1301 Farmville Blvd, Suite 104
Greenville, NC 27834

Published by Kravitz and Sons LLC.

ISBN: 979-8-89639-080-0 (sc)
ISBN: 979-8-89639-079-4 (e)
Library of Congress Control Number: 2025902008

TABLE OF CONTENTS

INTRODUCTION

My career in the medical profession and having worked as a registered nurse for more than 47 years, took me through many aspects of nursing including acute care in the hospital setting, to working 27 years in a general practitioner's office, to a short term in the correctional system and finally 10 years with hospice home care.

Working in the hospital addresses acute care, and the general practitioner office addresses patients with chronic or long-standing conditions that will usually get better and live a normal life, while hospice care addresses the direct opposite. The patients admitted to hospice are usually looking at death within 6 months.

My tenure with hospice home care was probably the most rewarding and gratifying as I developed close relationships with both the patient and their families during this crucial time in their lives. Many of these family relationships have continued to this day.

The following short stories reflect on some of the most memorable things that people may say—may see—or may hear as death approaches and oftentimes how their families are affected.

The old cliche that "Everybody has a story," subsequently everybody has a final chapter. Our story starts at birth and ends at death, and someone once said "the day we are born is the day we begin to die."

In this book I have written the final chapters for a number of family members, close friends and loved ones and, of course, a number of patients I cared for during my time with hospice. It will not take too long before you realize why I used "Going Home" as the title for my book.

I did not realize the first time I had experience with death and dying that it was anything more than a normal patient that had died a normal death until years later while working with hospice patients that I became aware and conscious of the unusual things that people may say, see, hear or do whether consciously, subconsciously or out of context. Death does not have to be painful or sad or scary. It can be and should be peaceful and calm and sacred if everyone is prepared and accepting.

The more I reflect on these final chapters, the more I realize I was in the presence of saints as they entered heaven, as the definition of a saint is a heavenly body or soul that has earned their way into heaven.

How much more blessed can I ever expect to be.

1

A PERFECT DAY

It was September, the season had changed, the days were cooler and shorter. It was time to start thinking about the soon approaching winter and Michigan cold temperatures.

The day started as it usually did when John and Elizabeth woke up at early dawn, said their prayers as they always did and enjoyed their breakfast. John helped Elizabeth with the dishes, as he always did, and then he went outside.

Since his retirement twelve years earlier John's day always started with a walk along the fence lines of the eighty acre farm to make sure the cattle were still secure. He fed the cattle and the chickens, and then he made sure they had plenty of water. While feeding the chickens, he decided to clean the chicken coop/brooder house and to put fresh new straw in the nests to cradle the eggs.

Next on John's list was to put his garage back in order. As a long-time and seasoned mechanic, there was a marked place for every tool and he expected it to be there when someone used it and returned it. He swept the garage floor and then scattered a thin layer of sawdust to absorb any spilled oil or grease.

It was lunchtime, so he returned to the house for some soup and a sandwich, to be followed by a thirty-minute nap. While he was eating his lunch, he shared with Elizabeth what he had been doing outside that morning, and that he was planning to work inside for the rest of the day

After his nap, John spent the next hour combing and brushing their faithful collie dog that had been their "best friend" for the past sixteen years. Their children had all grown up and dispersed throughout the world, only seeing them on special occasions for short periods. The grandchildren were growing up and everyone had busy schedules.

One last job as the afternoon was coming to the end, the oil stove they used for heating needed to be winterized and the soot removed from all the galvanized aluminum pipes—a dirty job, but it had to be done to prevent smoke, fires, and back drafts during the winter. To make the stove look new, the final step was to take old rags or dish cloths, smother it with coal black and a bit of liquid oil and then rub the entire surface down, making it shiny.

Day was done and he was tired. Elizabeth had fixed one of his favorite meals for dinner—scalloped potatoes and ham with custard for dessert. While they ate dinner, he reviewed with her that the cows were secure, the chickens had fresh nest and clean coop, the garage was in order, the collie had been groomed and the heating stove was ready to fire-up

Day was done and the evening was going to be just as busy. The Detroit Tigers were going to be playing a doubleheader with the Kansas City Royals, and they were being televised. Most people have ice cream in the evening, John and Elizabeth had popcorn every night. John popped a large bowl of popcorn, as he did every evening. As luck would have it, the Tigers beat both games. Everyone was happy.

It was late and time for them to go to bed. Elizabeth checked out the kitchen and made sure all the lights were off and that the collie was in for the night. John had gone to the restroom and announced that his bowels had moved. He felt good. Life was good. He had accomplished a lot that day— the home was ready for winter.

As he sat on the edge of their bed, he looked at His wife and asked if heaven was going to feel this good and if it was he was ready. He told Elizabeth he loved her, rolled over, had a massive heart attack, and went to find out what heaven was really like. It truly had been a perfect day.

Perfect for preparing the home for winter, perfect for dying and perfect for finding out what heaven was really like.

2
THE DREAM

S tella had been through a lot over the past fifteen years. She lost her mother and father to advanced age and dementia with Alzheimer's disease eight months apart. As an only child, she had cared for them in her home for eight years. Two years later, she lost her husband of thirty years to pancreatic cancer and her oldest son had been called to military service in the Army. Stella was a strong person with strong religious faith and knew that God would never send her more than she could handle.

Kenny, her oldest son, was now in his third assignment overseas as an Army officer. Her youngest son, Jimmy/Buddy was in his third year at the local university. He had decided to study locally so he could live at home and be with his mother and be able to help her with chores and upkeep on the house and property.

Stella and Buddy shared breakfast each morning before going their separate ways for the day. It was a Monday morning, the beginning of a new week, and the school year coming to an end. They were talking about what Buddy might be doing for a summer job to help pay for his education. The past couple of summers he had worked at the local hardware, and they had invited him back. Sounded good to both of them, he knew the store, they knew him, and he would not have to do something he was not familiar with.

There was a short pause in the conversation when out of nowhere Buddy asked his mother, "Is Kenny coming home?" Stella looked surprised and grabbed his hand, "Why would you ask me something like that? You know that Kenny is over there for at least one more year..."

It was then that Buddy told his mother that he had had a dream that night and Kenny was in it. In his dream, Kenny had come and was sitting at the end of his bed. They talked about his studies and how things were going. He had asked about his mother and how she was managing with everything that was going on, they were reminiscent about the times they had shared football games, baseball outings, and Saturday nights at the local grill.

At the end of the dream and before Kenny left he hugged Buddy. As he kissed him on the forehead, Kenny told him, "I will be coming home soon." And then he was gone. When Buddy woke up and looked around the room, he turned on the light. Kenny was nowhere to be seen, but it seemed so real.

After Buddy had left for school, Stella went to the fl,ile cabinet in her bedroom. The top drawer had been labeled. **Kenny**. In this drawer she stored all the cards and letters she had received from him over the last eight years. She had read them over and over many times.

In the drawer she was also storing various remembrances of his early years and school activities. His report card, his yearbook, his red and blue ribbons of acknowledgements in school, his merit badges from Boy Scouts. With these mementos, Stella had a spray bottle of Kenny's favorite cologne. When she would open the drawer, she frequently took the bottle and dispersed mist in the air to have him with her, so to speak.

As she opened the drawer this particular time, she was thinking to herself, "Did I forget something or overlook something in his last letter that said he would be coming home?" When she had read it over three times and found nothing, she pulled the previous two letters from the file and reviewed them numerous times. Nothing jumped out.

That was Monday, late Friday afternoon there was a knock at the door. Buddy was home and answered it. Standing in the entryway were three men in full uniform with the official formal letter from the USA Defense Department. Kenny was indeed coming home.

3

JOB WELL DONE

The call came into the office at nine a.m. A soft male voice said, "This is Walter, Anna has died, please come." I gave the message to the doctor, and he left immediately to go to the home where Walter was alone and met him at the door.

Walter appeared a bit nervous, very calm, and saddened. "Anna must have died in her sleep. I did not notice her being restless during the night and when I woke up, she was still in bed. She usually gets up before me, makes coffee and starts breakfast. She hasn't complained of anything, but I have noticed her slowing down, and resting more during the day."

The doctor did his initial examination, checked for vital signs, and estimated that Anna had probably died around eight a.m. At that point Walter said, "When I married Anna, I promised her parents and her family that I would take care of her for as long as she lived. I guess my job is done." To that the doctor responded, "Walter, you have done a great job."

Walter and Anna had known each other their entire lives. They were neighbors and had grown up together and went to school together. They had been married for seventy-four years. Walter was ninety-six and Anna was ninety-four. They had been farmers. They had raised five children, all of whom had graduated from the University and were now very successful in the field of education.

Before leaving, the doctor asked Walter if he needed help getting ahold of his children. Walter stated he would call his oldest daughter and she would take care of the rest. Doctor called the local funeral home and waited for them to come and remove Anna's body.

The second call came at seven p.m. from the family. Walter had died. When the doctor arrived this time, the family told him that after they had all arrived and Walter had updated them about their mother, he stated he was tired and wanted to take a nap before dinner. He made his way to his favorite chair and instantly fell asleep.

Walter never woke up.

The way I see it, even the Lord could not imagine Walter and Anna being separated for twelve hours. They had been partners for seventy-four years in life and now they would be partners in heaven for eternity.

Walter had done his job and the Lord did his.

4

THE GATE

Matthew had always been very healthy, at least that is what he told everyone and made them believe it. His philosophy seemed to be "If it ain't broke, don't fix it. If I am not sick, why go to a doctor?" It seemed to work for many years.

Matt was a local business man that kept him extremely busy for many years. He had a family and was very much involved in the community. Occasionally, we would be at a local restaurant eating lunch and sitting at the community table where "friends meet to eat." Knowing that I was in hospice care he would jokingly ask, "Will you be my nurse when it is my turn?" Matt was younger than me so I would respond with "You will probably outlive me!" Although I assured him I would be his nurse if the situation ever came To the surface.

Matt's turn came sooner than I could have guessed. He began losing weight, failed to show up at the business and was not coming to the restaurant for lunch. He made an appointment to see the doctor and have some testing done. He was diagnosed with cancer, but it was too late. It had already metastasized, and he was recommended to hospice care. When his name came to the admission board I immediately requested that he be given to me, as I had promised him I would be his nurse.

Matt's condition continued to deteriorate rather rapidly and he was unable to live alone as his wife had previously died. His only daughter from a neighboring town was able to move in and care for him, for as long as necessary. I was seeing Matt every day as there was a definite decline and weakening with each visit.

It had been six weeks when I received a call early one morning from his daughter stating that she had to work late that particular day and could I arrange my visit later in the day to check on him and offer him some soup or the protein drink. She was not sure just how late it might be before she made it home. I assured her I would make his visit my last visit of the day and that I would stay with her dad until she made it home.

Matt was sleeping in his lounge chair when I arrived. He appeared to be comfortable. He denied having any pain or discomfort, but voiced increased weakness. I did my routine exam and evaluation, noting that his blood pressure was barely audible and his pulse barely palpable. He didn't want any soup or protein drink, but he did take a couple sips of water.

We spent the evening reminiscing and talking about our families as I had known both his mother and dad as well as his grandparents and his siblings. As a local business man, he was familiar with my relatives.

As evening lingered into night Matt was getting more restless and agitated. He seemed to be having trouble sitting still, when all at once he said, "Maggie, I've got to go." I pulled the commode closer to his chair and managed to get him on it. He seemed to be fine and urinated a scant amount. He was done and I got him back in the lounge chair.

He seemed comfortable and satisfied for a short period of time when all of a sudden he said, "Maggie, I've got to go."

I responded, "Matt, you were just on the commode. Do you remember?"

Again, he said, "Maggie, I've got to go!" He was extremely restless and trying to get to his feet. At this point I gave him some of the medication that had been prescribed for restlessness and agitation, I attempted to pacify him by massaging his back and legs. I placed a cool cloth on his face and forehead. I offered him sips of water. Nothing seemed to work. I checked the Depends he had on and told him he could just go in the depends. He shook his head and repeated, "Maggie, I've gotta go."

He was quiet for about five minutes when once again he stated, "Maggie, Maggie, I've got to go. Please, the gate is open, they are waiting for me." It was at that second that I realized what he had been trying to tell me. As I looked into his eyes, I could see he was looking way beyond the room we were in. I also realized that in death, as well as in life, an urgency that intense needed to be fulfilled.

Realizing that death was not far away, the restlessness and agitation was worsening despite the medication. I told myself that somehow, I had to help Matt. I was alone with him, and he continued to try and get up out of the lounge chair by himself.

I closed my eyes, said a little prayer, and asked the Lord to be with me and to help me fulfill Matt's needs. Matt was a small man and since the cancer had eaten away at his muscles and body he barely weighed 100 pounds. He continued to try and stand, he needed to get to that gate. As weak as he was I was able to stand him momentarily, the total weight of his body on my arms, shoulders and thighs. He shuffled his right foot about an inch. I felt his body relax and go limp. I carefully lowered him back into the lounge chair. His eyes were closed and as I stood there and observed him, looking for signs of breathing and feeling for a pulse, he opened his eyes. With a faint smile on his lips, he looked at me and said, "Thanks, Maggie." That one inch shuffle was all he needed each the gate.

He closed his eyes, and as his body relaxed. Matt' needed when turned to the left and he took one last breath. Matt had made it to the gate, and to those waiting for him. He had been fulfilled.

My journey with Matt was over, I took a long deep breath and exhaled and an even longer deep sigh. I, too, felt fulfilled and satisfied.

I will never forget the look in his eyes when he said that last, "Thanks, Maggie."

5

TALK WITH JESUS

Rebecca or Becky as they called her was six years old and preparing for her First Holy Communion. She would attend preparation classes each week while her parents attended mass.

It was February and about 6 weeks away from the big day. Her mother and father had already bought her a special white lacy dress and matching veil. To go with this special dress and veil, there were shiny, new white patten leather shoes, a special white prayer book, a white rosary and her scapula. The invitations had been sent to their family and friends.

Her mother told me that Becky was excited beyond words. She would ask everyday, "How many more days do I have to wait before I can receive Jesus?" They would cross one more day off the calendar and this satisfied her, one day at a time.

Miss Joyce was Becky's instructor for the preparation classes that would last for 6 months prior to the special day. Each week they would learn and talk about Jesus and the Sacrament of Holy Eucharist on the level that a six year-old child could understand.

In her previous sessions with the children Miss Joyce had covered such topics as caring and sharing, loving and obeying your mother and father, as well as, all your brothers and sisters. She taught them the importance of living like

Jesus did in the Bible. They read stories from their children's bible each week. She taught them special prayers that would be used at their special event

The topic on the last night of Becky's life was praying and talking to Jesus every day especially in the morning when we get up and at night before we fall to sleep. She encouraged them to think of Jesus as their friend—their best friend—and that they could talk to him the same way they talked to their mothers and fathers, the same way they talk to their brothers and sisters, the same way they talk to their best friends at school.

As the session/ class was coming to an end, Becky raised her hand and made the statement "I will be talking to Jesus tonight." Miss Joyce agreed with her by saying, "Yes, all the children would be talking to Jesus when they say their prayers before they went to bed."

Becky was very excited and chanted, "I mean, I will really be seeing Jesus and talking to him tonight."

Miss Joyce again told her, "We will all talk to Jesus when we pray." Class was over and Becky's parents came to pick her up after Mass.

Fifteen minutes later the family was involved in an automobile accident and Becky was killed. Indeed, Becky would really see Jesus and talk to him just as she had said she would.

I had a chance to speak with Miss Joyce at the funeral. She was saddened and having a hard time believing and accepting what had happened to this special child. She shared with me that Becky had always been so happy and a joy to have in class. She loved to sing and she could get everyone around her excited and join in on whatever was happening at the time.

Miss Joyce continued by saying," If I had had any idea she was serious and understood what she was saying I would have shared it with Bob and Iris and possibly have delayed their return home by a matter of minutes. Perhaps the accident would never have happened and Becky would still be with us."

She continued, "The more I think about it though, the more I realize it was meant to be. Becky was so happy, so excited, and so joyful about seeing Jesus that night! How could I think of denying her that, and how could I ever think of denying Jesus of having her home as his friend?"

Becky was buried in her special white dress and veil, with all the accessories. The rosary was wrapped around her little fingers and the white prayer book was in her hands. With a smile on her face, there was no doubt "An angel went to heaven."

6

BEST FRIENDS

Beverly and Jane became best friends on their first day of kindergarten. They would later discover that they had been born on the same day, in the same hospital, and by the same doctor. Of course, living in a small community with only one hospital and one doctor, it was not unusual for most of the babies to be delivered by the same doctor.

Their family homes were about ten miles apart, so there was no reason for their paths to ever cross during their first five years. It was, however, "friends at first sight" when they met the first day of kindergarten. They remained best friends during their elementary and high school days. When it was time for college, they applied to the same university and were able to arrange to be roommates as well.

Upon graduation from college, their fields of education and their careers separated them and found themselves at opposite ends of the country. Marriage and raising a family kept them separated for the next forty years except for the holiday and birthday cards that were sent through the mail.

Their children all grew up, graduated from college, and were on their own. Eventually they both lost their husbands. They were both alone, but still on opposite ends of the globe.

The invitation for their 50th high school reunion party came in the mail. They called each other and decided they were going to show up and hopefully enjoy themselves.

It was as if nothing had ever separated them. Their conversation was as free flowing as it had always been. Even the classmates were surprised to hear they had not been together during all those years. They were just as carefree and fun-loving as they had always been. They had both aged gracefully with graying hair and a few extra pounds.

It didn't take long for them to decide that they wanted to renew their "best friend" relationship. They would each sell their homes, downsize all of their belongings, and buy a home together. Within a year all was done and accomplished. Their families were extremely happy that they could have each other. They would be perfect for each other and good companions in their late years.

They had been reunited for just over two years, living the good life, getting to know each other all over again. They bought a home in Florida, played golf every day, learned to play pickle ball and tennis. It was late afternoon, and they were riding their golf cart home from golfing when it was struck by a car. They were both tragically killed.

It has been said that the Lord works in mysterious ways, in a specific order and for a special reason

Divine intervention conceived them and arranged for them to be born on the same day. Family dynamics and circumstances separated them. Fate brought them together as best friends. Careers and family separated them. Fate reunited them, and Divine intervention arranged their deaths, and made them best friends for eternity

7

ON THE HORIZON

I got the call on a Friday, "Dad is home, Can you come? We need you." I assured them I would come as soon as my shift was over for the day, and by the time I arrived most of the family was already gathered.

The hospice supply truck had delivered the bed and hopefully all the supplies that might be needed. The hospice nurse had been there with the comfort pack. She reviewed the medications and how they were to be given to keep their father comfortable on his journey. She reviewed the oxygen machine and the urinary drainage tube. The family voiced understanding to the best of their knowledge.

When I arrived and realized just how grave the situation was, I asked the family to fill me in on exactly what they knew. The spokesperson told me Paul had been healthy and his normal self for four days, until all of a sudden he seemed to have pain all over. He was taken to the hospital, and after three days of testing and x-rays the doctor told them to take him home and call hospice, as there was nothing they could do to help him.

There were many questions from everyone present and realizing the shock they must all be in. I decided to have a Hospice 101 session. I started by telling them that their dad was dying and I needed to know that we were all on the same page with what was going to happen. Because of his rapid decline so far in the past few days, it would probably happen in the next day or two.

I encouraged his wife, the children, and the grandchildren to enter in his care if they were comfortable, to talk to him in their normal voice, to offer him drops of water and moisten his lips. I informed them that no matter how non-responsive he seemed, he could still hear them as our hearing is the last sense to leave the body. I ask them to share with their dad and the family what they had done that day and what they had planned for tomorrow. Anything to have them involved and feel more comfortable with what I knew was going to happen in the next forty-eight to seventy-two hours.

As the hours passed into the second day and then into the third day, I explained to them that as a person's condition declines we have what is referred to as a system slow down and then the systems gradually shut down. Many of them had already observed that the urine output was scant and getting darker in color. I touched upon the fact that his body would begin to cool down and the color would become gray and ashen as his blood pressure diminished and the oxygen levels went down.

We were doing great, everyone seemed comfortable and occasionally came to the bedside, holding his hand and whispering words of love in his ear, assuring him that they would be okay and they would take care of their mother. The family came and went throughout the day and evening as a number of them had chores to do at their own homes and farms.

Death lingered. It was the morning of the third day. Day was dawning and the sun was rising. A large reddish orange sphere could be seen on the horizon, it would be a beautiful day. The hospital bed had been set up in the living room facing the east bay window and it was perfect looking out over the pasture in the meadow below where the cattle were grazing. Looking closer one could also see two white tail deer standing at the edge of the woods.

Sitting at the bedside with my hand resting on Paul's chest, I felt the slightest movement. As I turned my head It looked as if he was trying to raise his head off the pillow that had been supporting his head and neck. I placed my hand at the base of his head to support it. He opened his eyes a sliver, squinted and mumbled "is that heaven?" I simply answered, "yes" and with that Paul surrendered to what he had seen on the horizon.

The one son had been standing at the bedside for quite some time, watching and waiting. He looked at me and asked, "Did I just hear him say what I think I heard him say?"

I nodded my head, and said "yes you did. You heard exactly what I heard." Everyone agreed that yes it would indeed be a beautiful day.

8

HOME FOR THE HOLIDAYS

Elsie had been fighting her cancer for seven years. She had survived three rounds of treatments and chemotherapy. She was tired physically, mentally, and emotionally. Her husband and family were drained. Recent testing, x-rays, and laboratory findings revealed that the cancer had spread to various parts of her body. The doctors advised them that more treatment and chemotherapy would probably not be any more effective.

Elsie and her husband Joseph talked it over. They had a family meeting with their 6 children. Collectively, they all decided there would be no more treatments and chemotherapy. Elsie hoped to have some "quality of life" days, no matter how short or long it might last.

Everything went well for 6 months. Elsie was able to go to her church, had an occasional dinner at the restaurant, went to a few of her grandchildren's sports events, attended a family wedding, and was planning for the holidays.

Little by little, day by day, Elsie realized her strength, energy and endurance were waning. Her appetite was gone. She was sleeping more. She needed more assistance with her daily routines and her enthusiasm for life went "out the window."

A visit with the doctor was set up for an evaluation. Because of her rapid decline in the past 3 weeks, the doctor advised and recommended she be admitted to hospice care in her home. This was done immediately as the doctor had informed them that the next three weeks would show an even bigger decline.

The holidays were coming and Elise's day had arrived. The family was all on board. Her vital signs were very faint, she hadn't eaten in days, sips of water less frequent, minimal response to stimuli. Her pastor had been called—prayed with the family and administered the last sacrament with blessings.

Day became evening, evening became night and Elsie continued to decline until there were very little signs of life. Her daughters had taken turns sitting at her bedside stroking her arms, rubbing her feet, combing her hair with their fingers, entwining their fingers with hers, laying cool clothes on her forehead, anything that might show they loved her.

It was getting late, and they began to ask, "How much longer?" That was my clue to explain the "here and there" phenomenon. As an individual approaches death, they often experience this and it is believed that they have one foot in the real world with their family and friends holding them here, and one foot in the heavenly world with the Spirit urging them to come.

They seemed to understand and agree. I explained to them no matter how close to death their mom and wife were, each time they touched her, rubbed her, talked to her, it stimulated her, and then she would have to "settle down" so to speak and get on with the job at hand—death was imminent.

At this point I ask everyone to leave the room as I knew they could not stay in the room and refrain from touching and talking to her. I am sure it was with great reluctance, but one-by-one they were ready and they wanted their mother to be at peace.

When all had left, I dimmed the lights and turned on the recorder to hymns and calming music. I repositioned her, made her comfortable, placed my chair in the corner at the opposite end of the room and I waited, not saying a word.

It took about an hour when she seemed to arouse a bit, trying to raise her head she whispered one word, "Jacob." The son she had lost 35 years previous in an industrial accident. The son she would be with for the holidays.

9

THE TIMELINE

In its early days and infancy, the word hospice was a verdict of death to 99% of the people that heard it. It usually meant that one would die in six weeks or less. It was difficult getting the doctors to admit patients to the program. They refused to make that prediction as it usually meant they had failed.

As time went on attitudes changed, protocols advanced, parameters were extended and doctors were admitting patients. The new definition for a hospice appropriate patient was anyone with a disease process or chronic illness for which there was no cure and from which the patient would never get better, and if the disease process or chronic illness followed the normal course of advancement there would be a decline every three months which was a certification period. It was the nurse's responsibility to show a definite decline in her observation and charting and maintain contact with the doctors to report the changes.

My first visit to Frank's home brought Amelia to the door and she greeted me with, "We have got to talk before you see Frank." She led me to the kitchen and offered me a cup of tea, and I accepted. I could feel her anxiety and fear. She was on the verge of tears.

We sat for a minute when she suddenly said, "I am not sure what you will be doing for Frank, but you cannot tell him he is going to die." I frowned and my eyes opened wide. I asked, "What has the doctor told him?" She responded, "Nothing." At this point, I informed her that he had a right to know if he were to ask.

She began to sob and her body was shaking. She reiterated, "I cannot allow you to tell him. He will give up and die right away. I am not ready for that." I hugged her and assured her I would say nothing unless he was to ask. She accepted this decision.

As I approached Frank's room and entered, I noticed the walls were adorned with pictures and memorabilia from his military days. I was to learn that he had spent thirty-three years in the military. He had fought in two wars, most of the time aboard a submarine. Three of the photos were of three different subs with newspaper articles of successful assignments.

A large shadow box displayed all the medals and stripes he had earned, including a Purple Heart and Medal of Honor. His official hat was perched on the chest of doors and his full dress uniform hung in the closet. He had worked his way through the ranks to become second in charge. Needless to say, it was an honor to be in his presence.

We talked briefly, I did my evaluation, reviewed his 776 medications, and discussed a tentative schedule for follow up visits. I sensed that Frank was getting restless and tired. I ended my visit and told him I would be back the next day. As I left the home, I told Amelia the topic of death never came up. She smiled and nodded approval with a thank you.

Frank did well for eight weeks, able to maintain his independence as far as his basic care, continued his radiation treatments for pain management once a week, was able to attend religious services, and even went to the golf course a couple of times just to hang out with the guys.

Gradually, his appetite began to dwindle. He started losing weight; his strength diminished. He was sleeping more, and was less interested in life in general. Amelia complained that he barely talked to her anymore, wasn't interested in the sports on television, had not watched the news in weeks. Before, he needed to see the news morning and night. I explained to her this was pretty normal as a person begins to decline. We again talked about discussing his decline with him and the imminent ensuing death. Again, she refused to allow me to bring up the subject with him. Again, she was still not ready, and hoping by some miracle he would get better and be cured.

It was a Tuesday and I had arrived for my usual scheduled visit. Amelia met me at the door and shared, "Frank says he does not want to go for his radiation treatment today. He had a bad night."

As I entered Frank's room, he was sitting on the edge of the bed looking out the window. I greeted him with, "Amelia was telling me you had a bad night and you do not want to go for your treatment today." He answered in the affirmative and shook his head. I explained to him it was his choice that he continue the treatment as they were for pain control and we could accomplish the same effect with medication.

Frank was concerned that they were expecting him in a couple of hours and I assured him I would call and explain the situation and put any future treatments on hold. He agreed and expressed his thanks.

Upon examination I realized there had been a definite and drastic decline since my last visit. He agreed and stated he had been feeling quite good until two days ago. We talked, and eventually he asked me, "Am I going to die?"

I nodded my head and said yes. He seemed relieved to know.

His next question, of course, was "When?"

I told him that would be hard for anyone to determine that, even the doctor.

"Do you have any idea how long it might be? I don't think Amelia is ready for me to go."

I assured him Amelia knew. We had discussed it a few times, and I had promised not to bring up the subject until you, yourself, asked me.

I sensed he wanted to talk more, so I said to him, "Frank, can you remember where you were and what you were doing two years ago at this time? How were you feeling?"

He thought for a moment and then said, "We were living here. I was golfing three days a week. My sons came for extended vacations, and we went fishing every evening. Amelia and I went to Florida for the winters. We were living the 'good life' so to speak. Life was good!"

Then I asked him to remember one year ago. Again, he said that things were great, he realized he was beginning to slow down and cut out some of his activities and related that to his advancing age. He was still able to do almost everything he wanted to, so no big deal. They had attended a couple of weddings and had made a trip out west to visit a brother.

I continued with my timeline and progressed to the past six months. His response was "Amelia and I had made the trip to Florida. It took us three days to make the trip. I was extremely tired and fatigued, and I never really recovered from that trip. We saw the doctor down there and decided to come home after two months. We could see the doctors here and have the necessary testing done...that was when we got the diagnosis."

"Two months ago when I came into your life, you were still getting up and around, going for your treatments, taking your own showers, eating at the table, watching your favorite programs on tv. Remember that?"

He answered, "Yes," and added," now I don't even care if I get up. I don't have the strength to go to the bathroom. I don't care if I eat, in fact, I haven't been out of bed since this morning."

We paused for a few minutes, not speaking, thinking about the timeline we had reviewed and how his last two years had evolved to the present. A couple of minutes passed and eventually he responded, "Knowing how the past week has gone, I could die tonight or tomorrow."

I nodded my head and shrugged my shoulders saying, "Only heavens knows when." He had figured it out himself with a little coaching from me. He seemed to accept the concept and possibility that death was near.

As I left his room and met with Amelia in the kitchen, I simply said, "Amelia, he knows," and then I shared the timeline I had used and told her he had figured it out himself. She wept for a period of time. Eventually saying, "I am glad. Thank you for explaining it like that."

Frank continued to decline on a daily basis and died peacefully in his sleep ten days later. He had served his country well, given thirty-three years of his life, and would be enjoying eternity with all his fallen comrades.

10
THE SIGN

William and Eva were modest, hardworking farmers all their lives. They had grown up together, schooled together, married together, and had been happily married for seventy-two years. Although they were never blessed with children, they had many friends such as their neighbors, their church family and the local farmer's association.

It was fall and the leaves had turned to their colors of red, orange, and yellow.

As I drove along the country road to their farm, I passed the two-track road that I assumed was their property line. A three-tier barbed wire fence encircled the entire property boundaries. Looking more closely I noticed small bird houses perched on top of every third or fourth fence post. They brought back memories.

Anyone who lived in the Midwest during the 1970's and 1980's remembers the DDT crisis when the overuse and misuse of DDT for mosquito and bug control also affected many of the small animals and the birds. It either killed them or they left the area, never to be seen for many years, especially the tiny pastel blue and yellow breasted bluebird.

Once the DDT was banned and considered illegal, it took a number of years to recover. Eventually the environmental agencies, the bird lover's associations and the local farmers decided that perhaps if they placed these little birdhouses on fence posts it would possibly, maybe, hopefully lure the bluebirds back to the Midwest region.

For forty years William remained diligent and each year he made six to ten new houses and placed them around the perimeter of the farm. No bluebirds ever showed up that he was aware of, no one in the area had ever seen one. Perhaps it would never happen or never meant to be again.

When I arrived and introduced myself as his hospice nurse, I mentioned the fact that I observed all his bird houses on the fence posts. He was eager to tell me his story and shared the fact that, so far, it had not worked and wondered if it ever would. He wanted to see one "before he left this earth."

As I did my evaluation, we talked more about his life as a farmer. He was easy to talk to, the kind of man you wanted to know more about. He told me a joke about the farmer and a peddler, we laughed, we shared a cup of tea and a cookie.

William was getting tired. His motor and engine parts, namely his heart, his lungs, his kidneys were wearing out just like the 1952 Farmall tractor sitting near the barn. The tractor had served him well for forty years, the motor and the engine that had been the heart, the lungs and the kidneys of his successful career in farming.

William continued to slowly decline and one-by-one he lost his ability to perform normal, simple activities of daily living. He was sleeping more, eating less, and lost interest in talking or seeing friends and neighbors. He was tired. His heart was tired; he was worn out. Eva was able to continue caring for Bill, as she sometimes called him.

Winter turned into spring and it was evident that Bill's time on earth was coming to an end. He had lived a good life as a farmer. He had fought all the battles that go with farming, but he never saw that one pastel blue and yellow bluebird that he had made homes for.

As he was dying and about to take his last breath, Eva bent over close to his ear and whispered, "Send me a sign when you get where you are going, so I know you got home."

Ten days after Bill had died and the memorial was over, I gave Eva a call to see how she was doing. I asked her if she felt up to a visit, as that was my normal procedure after a death had occurred, to see how the family was doing and to see if they needed anything.

She agreed to a visit and would be happy to see me. She instructed me to just give a knock and then walk in. "I will be sitting in the little breakfast nook having coffee."

I did as she had instructed. When I neared her I noticed a tear on her cheek, a smile on her face, and a quiver in her voice as she spoke. She looked at me and said, "Bill made it home." Surprised at what she said, I asked, "Really?"

She paused for a moment, gathered her thoughts and began to tell me that while she was sitting at the table having coffee a blue and yellow breasted bluebird appeared on the railing of the deck. It ran along the railing to the end, ran to the other end, turned around, came to the middle of the window, turned, looked at her, tweeted a few notes, then flew away.

Nodding her head, she turned to me and said, "I have to believe that was Bill's sign that he got home."

11

THE STORM

M y first awareness and experience with what people may say and do prior to death happened in the early 1960's. I was a recent graduate from nursing school and working in a small community hospital.

Rita was a sixty-three year-old woman that had recently suffered a heart attack, a.k.a. Myocardial Infarction, and in the 1960's a classic textbook diagnosis of myocardial infarction was a sure care plan that meant four to six weeks of total care, strictly confined to bed, total assist with all activities of daily living (ADLs). This included walking, eating, bathing, dressing, etc. anything that a patient may do for themselves in the course of day. The patient was usually always hospitalized for the first two to three weeks. Rita and her family had all been in conference with the doctor and the nurses, and stated they fully understood the care plan.

It was late afternoon, and I was making evening rounds with Rita's attending physician. It had been one week—seven days since Rita's heart attack. The doctor began by checking Rita's chart and reading the nurse's notes of the day, when Rita greeted him with, "I am thinking that I am ready to go home tomorrow."

The doctor looked up from reading her chart and said, "Oh really? We usually keep heart attack patients in the hospital for at least three weeks; you have only been here one week. Don't you like us here?"

"Oh, I like it here, and I have received wonderful care. My daughter was here earlier today and said my room is ready at home. They have rearranged all of the furniture, so that everything is close and convenient. My family feels they can meet all my needs and they really want to take me home and take care of me."

Finishing his evaluation and examination, he reviewed her chart and wrote his notes. As he was finishing, he told her, "I have ordered more lab work and an EKG for tomorrow morning, depending on the results and how they turn out, we will talk about it at that time."

Rita smiled and accepted the doctor's plan.

Later that evening Rita called her daughter and told her what the doctor had said and that she would be having lab work and a comparison EKG. She informed her daughter to bring her some clothing and shoes when she came to visit the next day as she felt certain she would be able to go home.

Her evening was uneventful. She visited with her roommate, watched the baseball game on the tv, read from her bible, said her rosary, as she had done every day for the past fifty plus years, a family tradition.

At 10:00 pm it was lights out. The nurse had given her the evening medications and a light snack. All was well in Rita's world and she was tired. She told her roommate this would probably be their last evening together as she would be going home.

Into the night, about 3:00 am there was a severe thunderstorm in the area and electricity was lost for a period of time. In the 1960's alternative electrical power was very limited and available for emergency use only. The storm lasted a couple of hours with strong winds and pouring rains

While the electricity was off, Rita suffered a subsequent heart attack in her sleep and passed away. When the lights came back on, the nurses found her peacefully gone with her rosary laced between her fingers.

Indeed Rita's room was ready—in heaven. Her heavenly family would be taking care of her—meeting all her needs.

12
THE BOX

Matthew was the youngest of six siblings—all boys. It seems like he was always catching up, making up, or trying to prove himself whether it had anything to do with sports, cooking, fishing, or hunting. After his graduation from high school, he enlisted in the Army like all of his brothers had before him with plans of going to college after serving his country in Korea.

Matt had been in the Army for six years when a ground bomb exploded about 100 feet from where he was standing. He was severely injured and lost his left leg and had multiple pieces of shrapnel fragments over his entire body. Because of their remote location, and with the war escalating around them, he laid in a tent on the battlefield for a couple of days. The medics on hand did what they could with their limited supplies. They were able to stop and control the bleeding.

By the time he arrived at the Army base hospital, he was in a coma and the wounds had become severely infected. He underwent multiple surgeries to repair the wounds, and remove pieces of shrapnel. After four weeks Matthew had developed a systemic infection throughout his body as a result of his injuries. His body was just not able to cope and one by one his systems began to fail and shut down. Matthew died on day thirty-two.

Matthew's body was sent home with his belongings that included a small wooden box with his name carved on the top, probably with his jack knife.

After the military funeral with full honor guards and his five brothers in the uniforms they had worn during their years in the Army, his mother opened the box as she found his tags, two medals of achievements, his jack knife, a little black book, the picture of him and his mother that had been taken the day he left for the Army, and the letter that never got sent.

The letter had been dated March 5th. Fifteen days before his official date of death on the certificate. As she read the letter her body began to tremble and tears rolled down her cheeks. It read:

Dear Mom,

I love you.

War is hell. I will not be coming back home to you and the boys. The doctors have done everything they possibly could do or expect to do. I am tired and I just want to go home.

Tell the boys I did my best. I hope they can be proud of me.

So until we meet again, remember that I love you.

Your son,

Matthew

13

THE BIBLE

Jessie was a simple man, a quiet man, a humble man that lived a very simple life in a small community and owned a very modest home. Jessie was always available to help anyone no matter who or what or when or where. He was the jack-of-all-trades and Johnny-on-the-spot when help was needed. It seemed as though he gave until the as no more to give and then he found a way to give again.

Jessie never married, so his immediate family was very limited as he was a transplant from Kentucky where his four siblings lived with their families. He was only able to visit every two or three years. Jessie had many friends—good friends who are often closer than family. He was sociable, agreeable, and fair. He always had a smile on his face and no one loved a party more than him, especially if there was dancing allowed. In the fifty-seven years I knew Jessie I never heard his voice go above a two no matter how frustrated, angry, upset or disappointed he may be with someone or a situation. It seemed he had a couple comebacks that he used, "What would the Lord say?" or "What would Jesus do."

Jessie remained faithful to the Roman Catholic faith of his parents and his childhood. He attended daily mass whenever possible. He was extremely active in the parish and eventually joined the Knights of Columbus, where he advanced through the various degrees. He was elevated and served as grand knight of the council for many years. After many years of service, he was presented with a new bible from the members of the council each of whom had signed it with a notable attribute that reminded them of Jessie. Some of the affirmations described him as a friend—companion—disciple—helper—giver—holy.

When Jessie showed me the Bible and we talked about it, there was a quiver in his voice as he told me he didn't know if he deserved the Bible as he said, "I don't really read the Bible that much."

I gave him a hug and said, "Jessie, you do not need to read the Bible. You know the Bible. You live the Bible every day, in every way, in everything you do."

He nodded his head as if to agree.

As Jessie advanced in age and was unable to live safely alone in his home, he was admitted to a senior housing facility. He was beginning to show signs and symptoms of dementia and Alzheimer's disease. I continued to visit him every couple of weeks until he passed away. I never made a visit that he did not greet me with a smile and a thank you for coming.

When Jessie passed away the readings at his funeral mass were appropriately chosen:

Paul's letter to the Romans tells us, No one lives for oneself, no one dies for oneself. If we live, we live for the Lord and his, and when we die we shall die with the Lord.

Psalm 116—I shall walk in the presence of the Lord in the land of the living. Matthew 25—I was hungry—thirsty—naked—lonely. What you did for the least of my people, you did to me,

As I listened to the readings, it was as if the Lord was saying, "I loaned him to you for eighty-seven years and now I want him back."

14
BUDDIES FOREVER

My scheduled visit with Howard was going as usual until his daughter, Anne arrived, as she always did, when she knew I would be there. We would exchange information and observations or changes that may have occurred in her father's condition since my last visit.

As she entered his bedroom, her first words were "Duke died this morning." Howard and Duke had been buddies for the past forty-five years. They fished together, hunted together, worked together, bowled together. Even though they were of different religious affiliations, they even worked on each other's committees! They had a simple understanding: if you help me, I will be there for you. They were a team and everybody knew it.

Howard immediately answered, "I know, he stopped by this morning."

Anne said, "What do you mean he stopped by? Who was with him? What time was he here?"

"He was alone. It must have been about 10:00a.m—right after I ate breakfast."

"How did he get here?"

"I am not sure. He came in through the kitchen like he always does, walked over to the rocker and sat down."

"What did you talk about?"

"The usual. The weather. The family. Our next hunting trip. He noticed the picture on the stand and we talked about the fishing trip when it had been taken. He didn't stay long. When he left, he said goodbye and that he would see me again later."

Anne looked at me a bit concerned and confused, shrugged her shoulders and shook her head. As she continued looking in my direction she replied, "That is about the time I got the call from his family."

Duke had suffered a very crippling stroke five years earlier and had been confined to a nursing home. His wife had passed away many years before and his family was unable to meet his needs in their home. Howard would visit him faithfully three or four times a week, often at mealtime and feed him. Anne was sure that Duke had never left the home after the day he was admitted.

At eighty-seven Howard had suffered a heart attack and was showing signs of senior confusion, memory loss, dementia, and early Alzheimer's disease, so Anne and I sort of dismissed it as such, even though Howard's tone of voice was very convincing and he spoke without hesitation.

We scheduled my next visit and wrote it on Howard's calendar as a gentle reminder.

When I arrived at my office the next morning there was a message from the on call nurse that night. Howard had died peacefully in his sleep during the night.

Duke had been right. He would be seeing Howard again soon—real soon.

They had been best buddies in life, now they would be best buddies for eternity.

Which again brings me to the old saying—The Lord works in mysterious ways—In a certain order—For a special reason.

15

READY FOR THE LORD

In my early years of nursing and while I was raising my family, I was involved with the REP program, religious education for the youth and young adults in the community and the parish. It was one way I could give back. I usually worked with sixteen and seventeen year-olds. We met once a week for two hours on Sunday evenings.

We would discuss and cover youth oriented topics with a religious aspect, as it referred to the church teachings. It was getting late into the program that year. We had covered subjects including the music they were listening to, the friends they were spending their free time with, their prayer life, parental relationships, dating, and death.

For the most part, I found that this age group have an appreciable amount of respect for adults in authority, could sit still for an hour or two, are eager to enter in the discussion if the topic is about them. Through the years I had all of my own children once or twice.

Over the years I found out and felt that sometimes where the participants are all the same age group, with the same problems and frustrations, similar likes and dislikes may be more open to sharing about certain subjects, that they may be hesitant to ask on a one-on-one basis, e.g. parent-to-child, mother-to-daughter- or father to son.

Eric was 16 years old, his whole life ahead of him, would be going into his senior year and talked about going to college to become a teacher. He was very active in sports and played in the band. He had always been very respectful and eager to enter into the discussions.

The topic on this particular night was death and dying, and the importance of always being ready. The Bible says we know not the time, the hour, or the day. I found that they were all eager to enter with questions and statements along the lines of:

"We are only sixteen; we are not going to die!"

"We are all healthy."

"We aren't going to die for years."

"I can't die... my parents need me."

As the time and the discussion was coming to an end, Eric raised his hand, stood up and said, "If God calls me home tonight, I am ready." The rest of the class kind of snickered and laughed, assuming he was just kidding.

At that point, I asked him, "Eric, do you realize what you just said? Do you understand what you just said?"

He repeated the statement, "If the Lord calls me home tonight, I am ready."

Again, at that point I told him and the class, "That is great. That is what we want to hear from our youth and our young people.

Class was dismissed.

It was Friday and there was an accident on his way home from school. Eric was killed. As I listened to the nightly local news, I heard his name. Chills went through my entire body and I couldn't help but remember the statement he had made four days earlier.

I remembered how he had made the statement with conviction and without hesitation. I truly believe he meant it and I truly believe he was ready.

16

THE ROSARY— THE CRUCIFIX—THE BIBLE

Barbara was thirty-three, the same age the Son of God was when he was crucified and ascended into heaven.

She had been a stay-at-home mom, but at the age of thirty she had returned to college to get her certification in Early Education Teaching. She was on the eve of taking her final exams when she realized her body was telling her things she was not prepared to hear.

A visit to the doctor and a multitude of tests and x-rays she was diagnosed with cancer of the skeletal system and her spine, with metastasis to other areas of her body. She was sent home with medication to help control the pain and maintain function for as long as possible. Shortly thereafter, she was confined to a wheelchair. A diagnosis of spinal cancer in the 1970s was almost always painful and terminal. Medication for pain and chemotherapy were limited and used sparingly. Hospice home care was not even in existence. She stayed at home while her family took care of her, along with people from their church, and a few neighbors.

During the next 9 months, Barbara would prepare her husband and her children for the time when they would be left without her. She loved her husband very much, as he loved her. She asked him to consider remarrying as she did not want her children to be raised without a mother. She had the talk with nine year-old Joey and told him he would be one of the men in the family and how important it would be that he help take care of his sister who was just four and one-half years old at the time. In her effort to prepare her daughter, she simply told her she would be going to heaven and becoming an angel so she could watch over her...When I visited a few weeks later, little Gina sat in the lounge chair with me. She looked up at me and said in her four and one half year voice, "My mama is going to die and go to heaven. She will be an angel and watch over me, so I have to be really good for my daddy and my brother." All the while shaking her head in agreement, and me wondering if it had been me in Barbara's situation if I would have had the strength and courage to do it so simply and beautifully.

I gave Gina a hug and replied, "I know sweetheart. Your mama loves you very much, and I am sure you will be good for your daddy and your brother."

During my ten day visit I was able to take her to the doctor's office for her scheduled chemotherapy treatment. I spoke with the doctor and he explained her current chemo medications. He promised me they would take care of her and do everything possible and available.

Barbara had been a member of the Angelus prayer group at her parish for a number of years, and during my time with her I was able to attend a session when they had the laying of hands on her head. Every member present would place their hands on her head and pray to the Lord for the strength, the courage and the grace to accept what the Lord was asking her to go through in the months ahead. The members were all aware of her diagnosis and terminal prognosis.

March of that year came around and her condition continued to decline at a rapid pace. At her visit to the doctor's office, he told them both that they had done everything that was available, nothing was working, her time was short. The Doctor told Willie to take her home, keep her comfortable with the pain medication, and to call him if she needed to see him and he would make a house call. Barbara gave the doctor a hug, thanked him for everything he had done for her, and said her goodbye.

It was Saturday. Willie had gone to early morning mass as he did every morning. Barbara was feeling tired, fatigued, and anxious. She asked Joey to take his sister outdoors to play and watch for their father to get home.

"She wanted to rest."

Barbara knew this day would come. She had known for 9 months. She did not know the month, or the day, or the time or the hour. 'Somehow she knew today was the day. Somehow she knew the time was now. She went into the bedroom and somehow she got her dress out of the closet, the dress she told her husband she wanted to wear for her burial, the dress she had worn the night they went to dinner to celebrate their tenth wedding anniversary. Somehow, she got it on. She sat on the edge of the bed and prepared to lie down. She picked up her rosary from the bedside stand with her right hand and picked up the small crucifix she had had since childhood with her left hand. As she laid back her Bible was on the pillow next to her head, the book she would read every night before going to sleep. She was tired, ready to accept her eternal sleep, her endless rest, her eternal rest.

When Willie arrived home, Joey told him, "Mama was tired and wanted to rest. She asked us to play outside until you got home." Willie entered the house and immediately went to the bedroom, opened the door, and saw Barbara lying on the bed. He realized his wife of ten years had died, alone, with the Lord at her side.

Years later, I spoke to Joey about his mother, what did he remember about her, what did he want to add to her story. He started by saying, "The day my mother died, I was the happiest nine year-old on the face of the earth."

I asked, "Because?"

He replied, "I realize I was only nine yrs old. I loved my mother; I know my mother loved me. She was a good mom. When I heard my dad say that she had died, I knew she would never have to suffer again. She would never again be in pain; she would never have to cry again, and I would never have to hear her cry again. I was happy for her and I know she went straight to heaven without stopping.

My immediate response was "Praise the Lord."

17

THE PROFESSOR

Guy had spent four years in the U.S. Air Force during WW lll and he had been stationed in Hawaii when the Japanese bombed Pearl Harbor. When his active duty service time was done, he returned home and finished his education with the G.I. Bill. He became a professor of science and started his teaching career at the local college.

It was by accident that he met Martha who was also a teacher. Martha had lost her husband in the war, leaving her with two small boys. Edward was four-years old and David was two years-old. They were instantly attracted to each other and over the next two years their relationship developed into marriage. Soon after, Guy adopted the two boys and raised them as his own. He taught them everything a son needed to know about fishing, hunting, scouting, camping, tending the yard, helping their mother, loving their mother, and taking care of her

The boys grew up and Edward went into education like his parents. David went into music and was teaching at a university in the Detroit area. David also played the cello in the Canadian Philharmonic Orchestral in Ontario. Neither of the boys had ever married. Edward lived in a nearby community and was able to visit quite regularly. David lived 300 miles away and because of his teaching career and his commitment to the orchestra his visits were few and far between.

Guy was seventy-nine when I first met him. He had been diagnosed with Non-Hodgkin's lymphoma which is a form of leukemia nine years earlier. He had smoked for a number of years and had some exposure to chemicals both in the war and in the science laboratory where he taught. Guy had also been diagnosed recently with debilitating emphysema and together they caused shortness of breath and difficulty breathing. The least bit of exercise, exertion and activity caused fatigue and increased weakness. The Non-Hodgkin's lymphoma had been controlled fairly well with medications and chemotherapy with the exception of an occasional flare up, but the combination of the two disease processes took it's toll on him. His condition advanced rather quickly and within six months he was homebound and bedbound. He was able to go to the bathroom and the table for meals and that took all his energy and stamina.

Martha was able to care for him and meet most of his needs. He had been admitted to hospice home care and the aid would come three times a week, helping her with bathing and allowing her to do necessary errands, go shopping, get groceries and have an occasional lunch out with friends. Edward was able to come frequently and help when needed.

It was late November when Guy's condition worsened and death was imminent. He had not been out of bed for a couple of weeks. Because of the increased shortness of breath he no longer had the energy to chew and eat. He lost all interest in reading the newspaper, watching the news on television which had always been a must in his daily routine.

A conference with Guy's physician determined that he was probably in his last three or four days of life. Martha contacted her boys and informed them of the doctor's prognosis. Edward came immediately, and planned to stay with his mother for his dad' s final seventy-two hours.

David, however, was unable to come right away. It was late November and holidays were approaching. The orchestra was set to have its first concert of the winter and the Christmas holiday. This particular concert was also to commemorate the tenth year of the current prime minister's term in office. David had met the Prime Minister a few times and considered him a friend. He called his mother and told her he would like to play in the concert and would come home as soon as it was over.

When you live in Michigan, everyone knows that when it comes to the weather anything can happen in a short period of time. As luck would have it, a snow storm developed during the performance. Six inches of fluffy snow fell with some collection of ice on the highway.

As soon as the concert ended, David started the long drive home. It took an extra two hours as it continued to snow the entire trip. Guy's condition continued to deteriorate and he was in and out of consciousness the last couple of hours. His vital signs were barely audible and palpable. There was minimal response to any stimuli—touch or verbal.

When David finally arrived, he stood at the bedside for a period of time—not saying a word, just holding his hand and rubbing his arm. Edward finally told him to talk to his dad, to let him know he was there. David answered, "He knows I am here."

Edward said, "No, he doesn't. Tell him who you are."

David looked a bit confused, but finally said, "Dad, it is David. I am home, and now it is time for you to go home. Ed and I will take care of Mom."

Though he was so close to death, the slightest smile on his lips appeared as if to say, "I know you will, son."

With that, Guy took one last deep breath and went home just as David had instructed him to do.

18

THE WINDOW

Mari Kateri was a Native American by birth with a heritage that spanned many generations. Her grandfather had been a chief and her mother an Indian princess. Mari Kateri's mother had married outside the tribe many years ago, but they maintained much of their culture, heritage, and customs. Her home was very evident of this with its decorations, knick knacks, moccasin slippers that she wore, rugs on the floor, paintings adorning the walls and blankets on every chair and bed. Pictures of her Native American family in their full dress, standing by the teepee with a totem pole that told the story of their heritage in the forefront. The jewelry box was overflowing with colorful necklaces and earrings.

Kateri, the name she answered to, remained active and current with her tribal heritage her entire life. She would often volunteer for many organizations and teach her Indian history and customs at the school and at festivals when requested. She had taught a beading class for years, making jewelry that would be sold at the annual Pow Wows..

When I met Kateri she was eighty-nine and had been dealing with congestive heart failure for a number of years. Her entire family was aware of her condition and the course the disease process would probably take as she aged. They were aware her daily functions would be greatly affected.

Their only wish was that she be able to stay in her home with her treasures. Hospice was initiated to assist her family in maintaining their goal.

Gradually, Katrei's condition declined and on the day she would pass away, she had fallen into a deep sleep. Her decline had taken five months, but now she had not eaten for the past three days, with only taking a few sips of water. Her pulse was very weak, and her respirations were very shallow. Cyanosis became very evident in her feet and fingernails. All signs that her systems were slowing and shutting down.

The family had all been made aware of her declining condition and that she was very near death. Ruth, her eldest daughter lived six hours away and was on her way. Anne, her eldest granddaughter, had been staying in the home with her.

Hours passed. Kateri was in no apparent distress, she appeared comfortable. All of sudden Anne remembered her grandmother telling her about an Indian belief that "we must let the spirit in so that our spirit can be taken and ascend into the heavens" Anne proceeded to open the window in the bedroom. We waited and waited. No reason why Kateri had not given her spirit up.

Ruth finally arrived. Anne met her at the door and exclaimed and told her "The nurse said grandma is ready and has been for hours. I opened the window to allow the spirit in."

Ruth observed the window opening, looked at Anne smiled and informed her "If you open the bottom part of the window to allow the spirit to come in, you must open the top panel to allow him to escape."

The top pane was opened and within seconds they again smiled as they observed Grandma's body had relaxed and submitted to the spirit.

I attended the funeral and burial a week later and it was definitely just as unique and dramatic as her death. It was held in a regular funeral home, but that was the only thing that was typical about it for me. Her family had asked me to sit in front with them and I graciously accepted the invitation. I had never been to an authentic Indian burial, and I was excited and interested in learning more about their burial ceremony. The atmosphere was very somber, sacred, and holy. Their native religion and customs were fascinating and Kateri would have been proud. Kateri was wearing her traditional tribal princess gown with colorful beads. Representatives from the tribe were numerous and in full tribal dress with head gear to match their various positions in the tribe. Four warriors with painted faces stood guard over the casket. The chief sat at the entrance to greet everyone as they entered. Traditional Native American music was playing with the rhythmic beating of drums in the distance. It was a memory I will never forget and will cherish forever.

19
ANGEL LADY

A lice was ninety-seven years old and I had been her hospice nurse for six months following a myocardial infarction with residual congestive heart failure. My nursing care plan was to follow her slowly declining condition. I was to keep track of her vital signs, her weight, her safety in her home, her needs, and to maintain contact with her doctor and report any changes. Many of the visits ended up being for companionship. She loved to just talk and reminisce about her past, her family, and her angels. Alice was able to stay alone during the day, but her nephew was there at night for her safety, should she have an accident and fall.

Alice was known as the angel lady by everyone that knew her or lived in her neighborhood. Anything and everything angel could be seen in and outside her home. Angels were present in every room of her house, even the bathrooms. She had them planted as lawn ornaments and amongst her flower garden. There was a curio case in the dining room with a village of more than 100 angels.

Alice had been taught as a young girl about her guardian angel and that it could be and would be her best friend. She had named her Gracie when she was 10 years old, and she would recite the special prayer many times a day. "Angel of God, my guardian dear, to whom God's love commits you here. Ever this day be at my side to light, to guard, to rule, and guide me. Amen." Her adoptive father once told her, "be a good girl all your days and the angels will carry you home."

Growing up her make-believe friend was Gracie. Her clothes were angel oriented, when she sent Christmas cards they had to have angels, as well as birthday and get-well cards. When she wrapped a gift nothing but angels was good enough. Is it any wonder that Alice did not dream of angels almost every night as she told me. At one visit she told me she had been dreaming of them quite often and at one point she saw them carrying her home to heaven. She laughed and said, "I really don't know what they are waiting for! My friends and my family have all gone home, what am I doing here."

Alice's mother had died when she was four months old after her appendix ruptured and caused a peritonitis infection in her abdomen. Peritonitis was a very deadly infection in the 1930's. Alice's father was left with three active sons, a two year-old daughter and a four month-old baby. As an active member of the Air Force and feeling overwhelmed, he didn't feel he could care for all of them. He decided to give Mary Elizabeth the two years-old and Alice up for adoption.

The girls were separated at this point. Alice was adopted by a family in the local community, and her sister went to a family in the city some 300 miles away. As soon as she was old enough to realize what had happened when she was born, Alice began trying to locate her family; she spent a lifetime searching. After many years she was able to locate the brothers and would reconnect with them and their families. She had never been able to find any information on Mary Elizabeth. Adoption records in the 1930's were sparse and often nonexistent.

Alice had prayed for fifty years, even Gracie could not seem to help her. Again, she would say, "I don't know what they—the angels are waiting for. All I want to know is where she is, is she okay, is she alive." Then out of nowhere it happened, Emma, one of her nieces was in college and taking a course on ancestry and genealogy. Her project for completion of the course was to trace her ancestry for four generations. Her DNA was sent to Ancestry.com and the link was able to locate her aunt Mary Elizabeth, who had passed away seven years earlier.

Alice was 98. She had found her sister. She was content; she was complete, and she was ready for the angels to carry her home.

Alice died shortly thereafter on the very day that Mary Elizabeth would have turned 100. The five brothers and sisters would be reunited and celebrated in heaven for the many lost years.

In closing—once again. "The Lord works in mysterious ways—in a certain order—for a special reason. He knows what He is doing."

20
THE PARTY

Emma was the life of the party. She knew how to get everyone else to join in. She played the piano—so to speak—self-taught as she had never taken a lesson. She played all the old favorites that people born in the forties knew by heart and would join in, whether or not they knew the right lyrics. Some just made up their own lyrics, as long as they fit the rhythm and the beat.

The mother of five children and grandmother of four, Emma had taught school for forty-three years and lost her husband twenty years before. Having recently retired, she was planning to spend the rest of her life traveling, spending time with her family, and volunteering at the hospital and the senior citizen center.

Life was rosy. She bought herself a puppy and booked a four-week cruise to Europe with her sister, who was also a widow. All the things she never had time for or had taken the time to do.

Almost immediately thereafter, before she was able to even enjoy or train the puppy, her dreams began to crumble. At first Emma shook it off as retirement lag and her body getting used to a new routine. Within weeks she lost her appetite and her weight was down twenty pounds—weight she could not afford to lose as she had never been a large person. Whatever was happening to the life of the party?

Her energy, her stamina, and her zest for life were gone. Emma's pain and discomfort intensified and a visit to the doctor and subsequent hospitalization revealed she was in stage IV of pancreatic metastatic cancer. Research and studies have proven that by the time an individual realizes there is a problem, it is already past effective treatment. A diagnosis of pancreatic cancer in the 1980's usually came with a short life expectancy of six months or less. Removal of the pancreas and transplant surgery was not an option at that time.

The family met with the doctor for a family conference to review the disease process, as there was no effective treatment available. The doctor and his team suggested admitting her to hospice care for palliative care and comfort.

Emma was admitted to hospice home care and that is when I met her. Her family were all on board with the hospice philosophy pertaining to comfort and quality of life goals. Her condition continued to deteriorate at a rapid rate and it was evident that she would never make even three months.

Four weeks after being admitted to hospice home care the family had a feeling she would never make it to the holidays, so they decided to celebrate early. A family gathering was planned with no presents—just eating—fun—pictures—singing and dancing.

The frequency of my visits for her care and comfort were daily by this time. I had familiarized the family with the signs and symptoms of systems shutting down and approaching death, and the procedures to follow. I assured the family, I would be there for them, and for her, when her time was at hand.

It was November 19th. I received a call from the family stating they felt Emma was ready and close to death. They requested I come and stay with her and the family until she passed away.

It was late afternoon when I arrived and confirmed that she was in her last few hours of life. The family had been able to keep her comfortable with the medication for pain, agitation, and restlessness. The family stated she had not eaten in the past twenty-four hours with minimal intake of water and ice chips. There had been no urine in the past fifteen hours. As I examined and evaluated her, there was no response to touch or verbal stimuli.

As the evening lingered, all the family had arrived and were anxious to help with her care and keep her comfortable. It was late—close to ten o'clock—when her oldest son made the observation and said, "Mom, there is a party going on in heaven tonight and they are waiting for you."

The family remembered and began talking about how Emma had three people close to her that had shared their birth date—her mother-in-law, her youngest daughter, and her college roommate, all of whom had previously passed away. Each year when November 19th came around there was sure to be a party somewhere, and they all knew that Emma had always been the life of those parties.

Emma continued to decline, her respirations were very shallow, her pulse weak and irregular. Her body was cool and clammy. Her color was dusky and gray. As we waited and oddly enough or perhaps prearranged in heaven, before the chimes on the clock in the hall struck midnight—Emma left for the party.

21

SPIRIT IN THE SKY

Jacob was eighty-nine and he would take his last breath in the same house he had taken his first. He had lived his whole life in a small community of about 1500 people. A community where everyone knew everyone for generations past and present. Jacob had married his grade school sweetheart, together they raised six children all of whom remained in the area and lived close by. His wife of seventy years had passed away five years earlier.

Jacob was known by most folks in town as Gramps and the young folks called him Grandpa Jake. Jake and his family had owned and ran the general store and combination hardware store for more than fifty years. He was a volunteer fireman, president of the local Lions club, and served on the school board while his children attended school. Jacob was affectionately referred to as the official unelected mayor of the town.

It was late afternoon when I made my scheduled visit, and it was apparent that he had declined in the past twenty-four hours. I had previously prepared the family that he was probably in his last days during my last visit.

Throughout the evening, members of the family arrived and gathered on the lawn, as the home was unable to handle everyone. Neighbors stopped by with food as everyone knew Jake and the pillar he had been to the community for generations.

I stayed in the house and sat at Jake's bedside. Occasionally one of the children would come in to make sure their father was comfortable. Jake died at 4:00 a.m.

It had been a warm summer evening. As I stepped out the door to let everyone know that Jake had died, the oldest son shouted," Look guys! The spirit has come to take Gramps home to the spirit in the sky." I looked skyward and it was as if the clouds had formed a halo and a moonbeam was shining through. My immediate thought was that of disbelief in what I was seeing, and then a chill came over my whole body.

It was almost as if on cue, the youngest brother picked up his guitar, started strumming and singing Norman Greenbaum's songs from 1969, Spirit in the Sky.

Soon everyone was singing. He had a friend in Jesus and now he is going home to the Spirit in the sky.

When I die and they lay me to rest, gonna go to the place that's best.

When I die and they lay me to rest, gonna go to The Spirit in the Sky.

Goin' up to the Spirit in the Sky, that's where I'm gonna go when I die.

When I die and they lay me to rest, I'm gonna go to the place that's best.

The music and the singing lasted for about five minutes. I had heard the song before, but I never paid much attention to the words. This time it was different. It was personal.

I was still standing on the porch steps, ready to make the announcement. As I looked over the gathering, I realized I had nothing to say, nothing to add. They all knew.

Gramps had gone to the Spirit in the Sky. Gone to the place that's best.

22
MAMA

Karen was the eldest of six siblings. She was the only girl with 5 rambunctious brothers. She was her father's little princess and became her mother's little helper. It was Karen's job to keep her brothers busy and out of her mother's way so she could get the household chores completed. Karen would playhouse with them, play school, and go outdoors with them. She became a tomboy, and as they grew up the boys were very protective of her. After all, Karen had taught them everything they would ever need to know. She was their little mother, their sister, their teacher, their playmate, their babysitter all in one.

When Karen turned 16 her parents allowed her to start dating and go to parties. They were very strict about her friends and her curfew time. Her mother would always say to her "Go have fun with your friends, make sure you are home on time and always make sure I know you are home by knocking on my bedroom door and say "Mama, I'm home."" Karen loved her parents very much and was always obedient and respectful of who they were.

Soon after she finished high school, Karen married and became a mother to five children of her own. They lived a very comfortable life as her husband had a good factory job and the children were all healthy.

In her mid-forties Karen was diagnosed with multiple sclerosis, a neuromuscular disease that affects the muscle tissue and gradually weakens the muscular system, leaving the individual handicap and wheelchair bound.

Karen's husband and their children were able to care for her for twenty-four years. Eventually, the bouts of flare ups were closer and the periods of remission shorter. When Karen became totally wheelchair bound and was no longer able to assist with any of her basic needs, hospice care was started to give her caregivers some relief and to help provide care and maintain her safely at home.

With hospice care she was able to stay home and out of the nursing home, which was the family's goal from the beginning. The children all lived nearby and were in the home frequently. Her husband had suffered a heart attack and was now limited as to lifting and exertion activities. A nurse aid was made available to assist with bathing and light housekeeping, allowing her husband some free time for himself..

Karen had reached the age of sixty-four and had suffered for twenty-five years, probably the average length of time for this particular disease process. It was evident that her multiple sclerosis had robbed her of her life and would take her life soon, far too soon. Many of her grandchildren and great grandchildren she would never know or even see.

I received the call from the family. They were concerned that something was different. They could not put a finger on what it was, but they had never seen her like this.

When I arrived at the home, it was evident that her condition had deteriorated since my last visit. Her family stated that she had developed a chest cold and was coughing the previous evening. They had put her to bed at her regular time and she had denied any real difficulty with her breathing or any pain. She had slept through the night and when they tried to arouse her they found her in her present condition.

As I examined her it was evident that her general condition and responsiveness to voice and touch were minimal. Her lungs were full and cracking. She was comatose and her body temperature was cooling down. The vital signs are barely audible or palpable. She was definitely at the end of life stage. A call to the doctor and he thought she probably had developed a pneumonia and her weakened condition caused by the multiple sclerosis made it impossible for her to cough and fight the infection.

The children had all been notified and were all present except for her oldest son who was a truck driver and was on his way home, but four hours away. Everyone was ready and hoping their mother and grandmother could be at peace.

The time passed slowly and Karen's condition continued to deteriorate. She was comfortable and in no apparent distress. Soon there was no readable blood pressure and no palpable pulse. I was not sure how much longer her heart and lungs would continue to function. Would she live until her son got home?

On schedule, her son arrived. Her family was complete as he made sure his mother knew he had arrived. His took her hand and kissed her on the forehead and said, "Mama, it's Jerry, I made it."

Though Karen had shown no response for the past twelve hours, she opened her eyes, looked to heaven, smiled and said, "Mama—mama I am home." With that, she took her last breath.

23
SANDY

Growing up as an only child on a small farm in the Midwest was no fun for Pete. He had no real friends as farming was a 24/7 job—rain or shine. His only real friend, true friend was his buddy Sandy, a golden retriever his parents had given him on his fifth birthday.

Living on a farm he could have had his choice of pets—horses, chickens, cows, goats, pigs, ducks, rabbits—they had them all, but nothing filled the void like Sandy. He was always there, waiting for him to come home. Sandy lived for thirteen years, and died the year Pete graduated from high school. "He was the best. No one or nothing can ever replace him."

Upon graduation, Pete enlisted in the Marine Corp. He was ready to give up his 24/7 job, see the world, have some fun, make some friends. When boot camp was done, he was sent to Vietnam where he spent the next six years. Pete was fortunate and came home with no major injuries, many of the friends he had made were not as lucky. Once again, he lost his best buddy, not just once, but three times during those six years.

When his time with the Marines was over, Pete joined a country western band—singing and playing the guitar. He wrote many patriotic songs and hymns about his life in the service, the war, and the small farm he had left behind. He longed to go back to that farm, but it was long gone as it had been auctioned off to settle the estate after his father's death.

Pete had been around the block a couple of times as he used to say. The twenty-five years he had spent on the road with the band scattered his children in four different states. He was away from home a great deal of the time, so he was never really close to them. He barely knew them, some of the grandchildren he had only seen once, maybe twice. As the years between them lengthened, it was just easier to excuse the absence of them in his life as too far to travel, or they were too busy to come and see him. He settled for a small piece of land in the country, remembering the small farm he left behind many years ago.

Pete had always been quite healthy, having been raised on a farm and spending six years in the service, he was accustomed to healthy eating and exercise. By the time he reached the age of sixty-eight though he was having problems with breathing. He was diagnosed with emphysema and pulmonary insufficiency along with an adult form of leukemia, the residual effects of smoking two packs of cigarettes per day and chemical warfare used in Vietnam. It was necessary for him to be on oxygen continuously.

It was difficult for him to accept the fact that he could no longer be Pete. He became frustrated with himself and the world in general. He didn't want people coming around. He didn't want his family to know, didn't want to burden them, didn't want to see it on their faces, or hear it in their voices. Because of the many years he had spent on the road, he had never made many long-standing friends or developed close relationships. History seemed to have repeated itself already a couple of times and he would probably lose any "best buddy" anyway.

When I first met him, Pete tried to maintain his macho man image and was determined to get better, "Nothing was going to get him down." By this time, I had eight years of hospice experience and knowing and understanding the severity of his diagnosis, I began to wonder if I would be able to see him through this most difficult period in his life.

Over the next four months, as his disease process robbed him of his energy, his strength, his courage, and his patience, he mellowed and we were able to talk about the inevitable— end of life. He shared with me that he had never been very religious, but he did believe in the Lord and a place called heaven. He agreed to have his wife call his children and have them come to visit. One-by- one they each showed up and they were able to accept each other for who they were and what they were. The past was "water over the dam."

On the day that was to be Pete's last, his wife called early in the morning and stated he had been very restless all night. She had given him the medications with minimal relief. Upon arrival at the house, it was evident that Pete was near death. The increased agitation, restlessness, and anxiety was known as the one foot in this world and one foot in the next. I touched his arm and said his name, he squinted a bit, recognized me and stated, "I am ready, Please Lord, take me home."

I elevated the head of his bed slightly to help his breathing. Violet was sitting on a chair at the side of his bed. My concern and goal was to keep him comfortable by giving him the medication and changing his position. He seemed to be comfortable. There was no moaning or groaning. There was no frowning or expression of pain on his face. All of a sudden, out of nowhere in a very weak voice he said, "Sandy" and then as a question, "Sandy?" As I looked at his face and his eyes, it was evident he was seeing something beyond us.

He attempted to coach Sandy to come closer with his fingers. Then he added, "Sandy came to take me home."

That was the last thing he said, he took his last breath and went home with his buddy, and as we all know, according to Walt Disney, "All Dogs Go To Heaven."

24

THE ROOM

Raymond had been an auto mechanic and used car salesman his whole life. He had met his wife in Germany during the war and they were married over there. After the war they migrated to America where they started their family and raised three daughters.

As a child, Ray suffered from asthma and allergies. He was raised in the Midwest farming region and it seemed he was allergic to everything e.g. dust, hay, molds, wheat, pollens, resulting in frequent exacerbations of the asthma. He took allergy injections and medications for years, but over the years his lung tissues became scarred and his respiratory function was diminished. Often a flare up of his asthma would lead to pneumonia and additional scarring of his lungs.

Raymond had learned to live with his condition and by avoiding certain activities, weather changes, excessive exercises, running and seasonal changes, with his medication and not smoking he lived a normal life for sixty years.

In his mid-sixties he developed emphysema and chronic obstructive pulmonary disease with congestive heart failure. To complicate things even more, Ray developed signs of early dementia in his mid-seventies.

Judy, Ray's wife, had learned to live with and cope with the breathing problems, but when the dementia developed, she was overwhelmed and needed some help. Their daughters could help to a certain point, but they all had jobs and were raising families. They were there on weekends, so hospice care was initiated for additional help and support.

Gradually and over a period of time his disease processes, all of them, progressed to life threatening status. Raymond and his family slowly realized things were never going to get better. Together they made final arrangements and we reviewed the signs and symptoms of "End of Life."

Every individual and every family are different as to how much they are willing to accept death, and how open and willing they are to talk about it. Everyone seemed ready and willing and they found out that the more they talked about it the easier it was. They found out that Raymond didn't want to die before his turn, but that he was ready and not afraid. His wife and daughters assured him they would be fine and take care of each other.

On the evening that was to be his last, the family had called and informed me that his breathing was very labored and the medication was giving him minimal relief and comfort. When I arrived it was evident that his condition had declined drastically in twenty-hour hours. He was experiencing all the signs and symptoms of approaching death. He was extremely restless and anxious and because of his severe respiratory problems everything was more pronounced. He was having difficulties lying down even though the oxygen was at the maximum and the head of the bed was elevated all the way.

As the evening advanced and the family had all gathered, the eldest daughter was sitting at the bedside and began to talk to him and told him his time was at hand. She told him the Lord was preparing his room and it would soon be ready. Judy turned on a small subdued lamp and soft music of hymns, sat at his side and caressed his arm and face. Raymond was able to relax somewhat.

It took approximately three hours and soon his vital signs were nonexistent and his respirations very shallow. I motioned to his daughter that his time had come, she immediately said, "Dad, your room is ready. Can you see your room Dad?"

Though he had been unresponsive for at least three hours, Raymond opened his eyes wide and stared at the ceiling in the far corner of the room. His eyes were fixed and glowing and he said one word, "yes." With that he took one last breath and went to his room.

With a smile on their face and a tear on their cheeks, the family appeared at rest and satisfied. Dad had found his room in heaven.

25
"YUP"

He was not the smartest kid in the room, but he definitely was the funniest, the class clown, and who doesn't love a clown. He told it like it was and he didn't mess with words. Marty was a tower of strength and energy, always ready for a good game of cards, a polka dance or a competitive game of bocce ball. Someone once said, "perpetual persistent optimism is a perpetual positive force multiplier." and that was Marty. No matter how bad or dismal things might be, they were bound to get better, and they usually did over a period of time. The sun always came out tomorrow.

Marty had recently retired after working forty years at a woodworking factory that was known for their religious furniture and accessories including pews, kneelers, crucifixes, statuses, Bible stands, chairs, and altars. He had advanced over the years from cutting the wood to staining and painting to management. Marty was a good worker, a team player, a positive force. Marty liked everyone and wanted to give everyone a chance. Everyone liked Marty and wanted to be around him.

Marty loved a party. If there was a party, he was there, especially if there was dancing. He loved to poplka and he was a personal friend of the Polka King, Frankie Yankivic. His family followed Frankie's band for years. There was never a dull moment with Marty around. He and his wife danced every dance, fast or slow, didn't matter. He may not have known the correct steps to whatever dance they were doing, but he kept step and time to the music and nobody was the wiser.

Marty was fifty-nine years of age, in his prime and ready to spend more time at home and in the family blueberry fields that his father-in-law owned. He was a picture of health most of his life. As midlife crept up he developed hypertension and diabetes. He had been a smoker in his twenties, but had given it up thirty years previous.

The family reunion came around that year as it always did the third weekend in July. Marty was there with all his jokes and stories, and handing out licorice. The kids loved him as he played with them all. Marty and his wife had never been blessed with children, so all the children became theirs overtime.

Three weeks later Marty was feeling under the weather and had a cough and upper respiratory infection. A trip to the doctor's office revealed he had pneumonia and pulmonary fibrosis, residual effects of the forty years of exposure to the paints and lacquers used at the shop.

His disease process came on very suddenly and advanced very quickly. He had been up and about enjoying family activities one weekend and three weeks later he appeared to be on death's doorstep. The pneumonia and the pulmonary fibrosis lead to congestive heart failure, and immediately the kidneys began to shut down. When the kidneys begin to fail and shut down, the toxins remain in the body and systems begin to slow down and shut down vital organs.

I visited Marty at the hospital and as I entered his room I was greeted by machines and tubes connected to every orifice and opening of his body. He was semi-comatose and, as I was squeezing his hand, there was no reaction. I stayed for approximately an hour, talking to him like I would normally if I had gone to his home for a visit. I assured him I would be back tomorrow, and hoped he would be better.

As I was leaving, I spoke with the nurse in charge and she stated his condition was grave and the doctor was not sure if he would survive. She reviewed his chart and pointed out that he had two strikes against him with the pulmonary fibrosis and congestive heart failure, now the pneumonia complicates everything. Not sure if his heart and lungs had enough power to fight it.

When I arrived the next day, the head of his bed was elevated and his eyes were open. I greeted him, "You sure look better than you did yesterday when I was here. Do you remember me being here?"

He answered, "No, not really." He paused, and then continued, "I'm going home tomorrow."

I responded, "Oh really. What does the doctor say about that?"

He answered, "I haven't told him yet."

I pointed to all the machines and tubes coming from all over and I said, "Once we can get rid of some of these tubes and machines, we can start thinking about going home."

With that he replied, "Yup, I am going home in the morning." He sounded very sure and convinced of what he was saying.

Was he saying it consciously or hopeful thinking? I wasn't sure.

Then he added, "It's all in the hands of the Lord. He will figure it out and arrange all the details."

When I left that day he was resting peacefully. I had assured him I would be back the next day and if indeed he went home in the morning, I would visit him at home.

He responded, "Yup." His usual statement or answer to everything.

His wife, Alice, had been there all afternoon and evening and stayed until visiting hours were over. He continued to do well that day, so when her ride arrived to take her home, she kissed him goodbye, and said she would be back in the morning.

It was 3:00 a.m. when the machine's alert buzzers went off. Marty had taken a turn for the worse. His body had no defenses left to fight the pneumonia and indeed he went home. It was tomorrow and it was morning just like he had predicted, and I have to assume the Lord had taken care of all the details.

26
THE FACE

Paul was three and a half years old when his father died and whenever anyone asked him if he remembers his father, it was always a "kinda, sorta," maybe response. He knew there had been someone in his life that was no longer there. He remembered playing with someone. He remembered running and laughing and giggling. He remembered hide and seek. He remembered peek-a-boo, but he was never able to connect all the dots despite the many pictures and souvenirs his mother had around the house.

After a few years Paul's mother remarried, and he became the eldest of three siblings. He was eventually adopted by his stepfather, as he was the only father he had ever known. They lived very comfortably in a small country community on an eighty-acre farm. Growing up Paul and his brothers learned the art of hobby farming, living off the land and self-sufficiency.

Paul spent a number of years in the Navy serving his country in Vietnam and the Gulf Wars, where he learned to be an auto mechanic. Upon returning home and leaving the Navy, Paul married, bought himself a small farm and opened his own auto mechanic garage and parts business. He was the typical hobby farmer with a job in the city. Eventually they adopted a son as they were never blessed with one of their own.

In his mid-seventies and after forty-five years in the auto business Paul decided to retire, live the good life and returned to his hobby farming full time, with hopes of selling his produce.

Paul and his wife had always been very conservative and self-sufficient, able to take care of their needs and necessities. There had never been a situation or illness they could not take care of using their parents and grandparents home remedies. Paul had not seen a doctor in over forty years, since he got out of the Navy. His theory was, "if it ain't broke, don't fix it. Let the doctor take care of people that are sick and need him."

It was mid-autumn, the leaves were falling and the weather was changing. The lawn needed to be mowed and groomed one last time. While trying to start the mowing machine that Paul had been using for at least ten years, his right arm shattered without injury. A trip to the Doctor and hospital revealed cancer of the bone. A diagnosis of carcinoma of the bones with metastasis throughout his body was made and confirmed. Prognosis very poor.

Upon admission to hospice and while reviewing his chart and medical records it was hard to phantom and imagine the extent of pain and discomfort he must have been experiencing to reach this point without having admitted to or acknowledging it. Once again his theory was "I figured it was part of aging and getting older, possibly the weather, working in various positions and situations, many hours. I was never not able to function."

Because of the advanced disease process and poor prognosis Paul's condition declined rather rapidly and soon he was confined to his home and a wheelchair. He was unable to walk and found it easier to sleep in a recliner that was electric and would get him up and down with less effort and discomfort. The family was very supportive and ready to assist in any way.

Within weeks Paul had lost a considerable amount of strength and energy and it was evident he would not see his next birthday which was eight weeks down the road. Together his family discussed his death and made final arrangements. Paul had never been a frequent or regular churchgoer but he believed. He believed in the Lord and a life after death. A local minister agreed to officiate at his service and memorial.

Death was at the door and Paul lapsed in and out of consciousness and awareness, opening his eyes briefly when aroused. The family was able to keep him comfortable with medications that had been increased appropriately for pain and discomfort. The furniture in the room had been rearranged to allow maximum space and easy access for his family and caregivers. A small lamp was placed in the far corner of the room to provide a subdued light that is believed to attract the spirit as

It enters eternity. Soft music and hymns had been playing to also help Paul relax.

Ken, Paul's younger brother spent time with him during his last 72 hours, and as death approached he had observed that when Paul was aroused for whatever reason he would point to the lamp and the light, as if to be reaching for something or someone. As time passed and the closer Paul was to death, the more convinced and sure his brother was seeing someone he knew and felt there was an occasional faint smile on his face. Finally, out of the blue Ken looked at me and said "Maggie, I think he sees his dad and he is remembering him as he knew him at three and a half years of age."

At the moment of death Paul opened his eyes one last time, his eyes were glistening and indeed there was a smile on his face. I believe he had finally found the someone that had been in his life, the face he had been searching for the past seventy-two years.

At the moment of his death Paul had been able to connect all the dots.

27

THE BLIND WILL SEE

Phillip had been completely blind for the past ten years.

It all started when he was 10 years old when he and his twin brother were target shooting with the B-B guns they had received for their birthday. They knew all the rules and were following them, but somehow one of the pellets ricocheted off a tree and hit Phillip in the right eye. Growing up in the early 1930's there was no surgery available to correct this type of injury. All one could hope for was that no infection set in and cause further damage and complications. The doctors all encouraged him by reminding him that research shows and has proven that ten percent of people he knew probably were only seeing out of one eye, and not to worry about the things he could not see, but to be thankful for the things he could see.

Despite Phillip's visual handicap he was able to fulfill his dreams of becoming a very successful farmer as his father before him. He was able to raise his family of five children on his two hundred acre dairy farm. They were all able to go to college and graduate with degrees, when college was affordable and families did not have to remortgage their farm 5 times over.

At the age of seventy Phillip developed a viral infection in the left eye that left him totally blind over a period of time, despite all the medical interventions available in the nineteen eighties. Completely blind he was able to function minimally with the help of his wife and the son that lived with them

By the time Phillip reached the age of eighty he began having problems with his breathing and a diagnosis of respiratory edema with emphysema was made following testing and x-rays that showed scarring of his lung tissue resulting from years of smoking the pipe, breathing in dust from the farming, weed killing agents and inhaling fertilizer fumes. Before long he was forced to use oxygen all the time, as his lack of appropriate and sufficient air exchange robbed him of his strength and energy.

Eight weeks prior to his death Hospice care was initiated into the home to help manage his end of life care, provide needed medications and equipment to keep him comfortable and to assist the family and inform them of the probable path the emphysema might follow as he continued to decline. One by one his systems began to slow down, his kidneys and the amount of urinary output, his digestion as he didn't have the strength and energy to chew and eat, his lungs despite the continuous use of oxygen, his heart with fluctuating vital signs and generalized cyanosis. The skin felt cool and clammy to touch, all signs of approaching shutdown.

Phillip's day of death was at hand. I made a visit early in the morning. Everyone was comfortable and on board with what would happen in the next few hours. Phillip appeared to be comfortable and in no acute distress. There had been no measurable amount of urinary output since my last visit. Family stated minimal amount of water and ice chips taken in. His blood pressure was very low, pulse irregular and weak, respirations shallow.

Phillip continued to decline over the next three hours and suddenly he opened his eyes, had a look of shock on his face, "I can see, Emma, I can see you, Emma, your blue dress, your green." With that he was gone. His body relaxed—his heart stopped—his breathing ceased. Emma told me the green he never finished was referring to her green eyes that he always teased her about from the moment they met. With a smile on her face and tears rolling down her cheeks she sat at the bedside holding his hand until the undertaker came, not wanting to let go.

It is believed by many that at death as we enter heaven our handicaps and earthly imperfections will be made perfect and our earthly bodies will be as pure as fresh fallen snow. The lame will walk—the deaf will hear—the blind will see.

CONCLUSION

The Baltimore Catechism teaches us that God created us to know him, to love him, to serve him on this earth so that we can be happy with him forever in heaven. It also teaches us that the Blessed Trinity is three persons in one. God the Father who created us, God the Son who saved and redeemed us and God the Holy Spirit who is the essence and ever presence of God the Father and God the Son within us as we live our daily lives. To the extent that we allow the Holy Spirit to work within us and through us. I feel is a barometer of the extent that we know, honor, love and serve the Father and the Son, our creator and our savior.

To every beginning there is an ending. To every birth there will be a death, some lasting a long life and some tragically cut short due to illness or accidents. Our birth starts the first chapter in our lives and our death finishes the last chapter. The day we are born is the day we begin to die.

Everyone is a unique individual with unique qualities, traits and personalities. Our lives are patterned, affected by and influenced by familial traditions, our heritage, our culture, our environment and often our faith. The way we have lived our daily lives over the years is frequently apparent and reflected at our death.

With the help of the Holy Spirit in my life, guiding me, inspiring me and influencing me along the way during my years of nursing, especially the ten years I spent in hospice care, I have been able to write this collection of short stories and share what an individual may say, see, do or hear on their journey from life into death.

Finally, I wanted to stress the constant and ever presence of God the Father, God the Son and God the Holy Spirit and their subtle control of our lives from birth through death. Death should not and does not have to be something scary or fearful. Death can be calm, peaceful, holy and sacred.

Thank you for reading my book and I hope you enjoyed it.

Praise the Lord.